Jackson AND Bud's BUMPY RIDE

America's First Cross-Country Automobile Trip

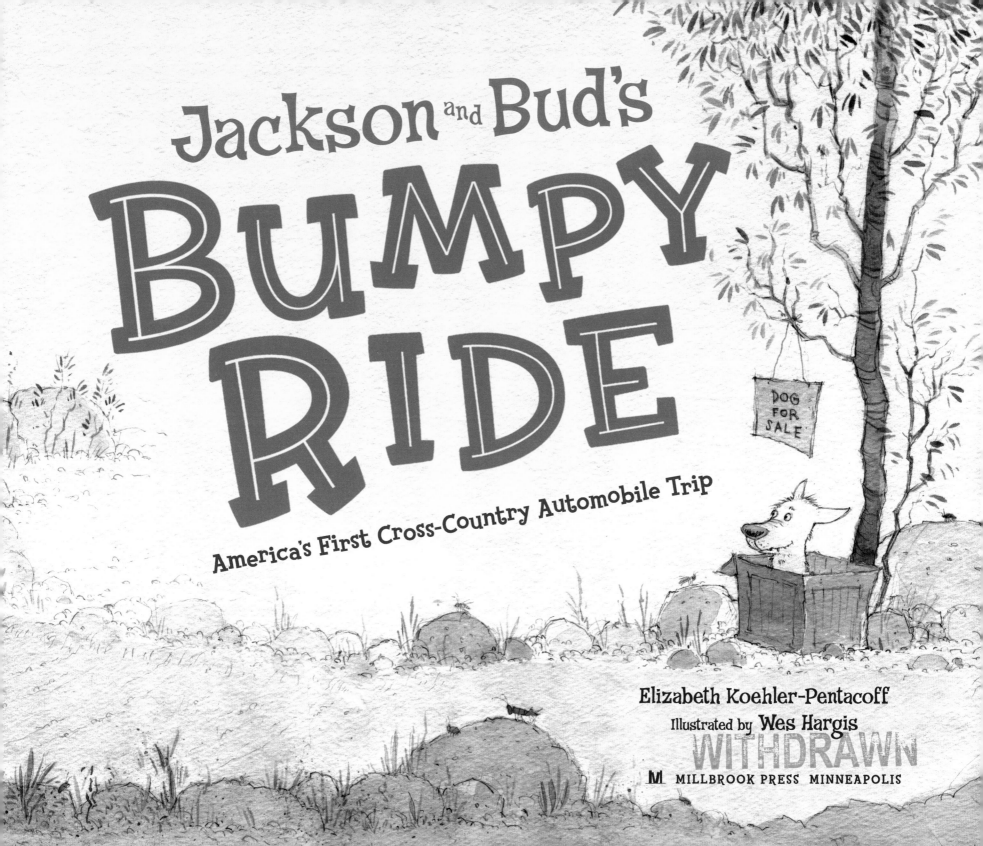

DOG FOR SALE

Elizabeth Koehler-Pentacoff
Illustrated by **Wes Hargis**

M MILLBROOK PRESS MINNEAPOLIS

For my good friend Ellen
And with special thanks for Jean
—E.K.P.

For Debbie
—W.H.

The author wishes to thank the Tacoma Public Library and the University of Vermont Library.

The photographs in this book are used with the permission of: courtesy of Western Reserve Historical Society, Cleveland, Ohio, p. 34 (top); Special Collections, University of Vermont Library, pp. 34 (bottom), 35 (both).

Text copyright © 2009 by Elizabeth Koehler-Pentacoff
Illustrations © 2009 by Wes Hargis

Millbrook Press
A division of Lerner Publishing Group, Inc.
241 First Avenue North
Minneapolis, MN 55401 U.S.A.

Website address: www.lernerbooks.com

Library of Congress Cataloging-in-Publication Data

Koehler-Pentacoff, Elizabeth.
    Jackson and Bud's bumpy ride : America's first cross-country automobile trip / by Elizabeth Koehler-
  Pentacoff ; illustrated by Wes Hargis.
       p.   cm.
    Includes bibliographical references.
    ISBN 978-0-8225-7885-7 (lib. bdg. : alk. paper)
  1. United States—Description and travel. 2. Jackson, Horatio Nelson, b. 1862—Travel—United States. 3.
Automobile travel—United States—History—20th century. I. Hargis, Wes, ill. II. Title.
E168.K733 2009
917.3—dc22   2008012752

Manufactured in the United States of America
1 2 3 4 5 6 – DP – 14 13 12 11 10 09

MAY 19, 1903 ○ THE UNIVERSITY CLUB
SAN FRANCISCO, CALIFORNIA

"I bet fifty dollars no one can ride in a horseless buggy across America," says a man.

Horatio Jackson sits up straight. *Of course it can be done,* he thinks. *Those new automobiles can do anything.*

"I bet someone can do it," he says. "*I'll* drive from California to New York in less than three months!"

The wager is on.

As the twentieth century began, horses pulling carriages ruled the road. Most people didn't think autos would ever replace them. Jackson wants to prove the automobile is the country's future.

Jackson hires a mechanic named Crocker, buys a used 1903 Winton auto, and he's on his way. He calls his automobile the *Vermont*, after the state where he lives.

MAY 23 ● SAN FRANCISCO, CALIFORNIA

"Good-bye! Good luck! Be careful!"
shouts Jackson's wife, Bertha, who will
be returning to Vermont by train.

"Don't worry, my dear," Jackson pats the
car. "This trusty machine will get
us there with no troubles at all!"

About fifteen miles later . . .
**Bump, bump, bump.
Ka-plooee!**

"Just a momentary delay," says Jackson. He whistles and kicks the other tires. "The other wheels are fine!"

The men travel on through California. They drive through purple fields of lupine. In the Sacramento Valley, the auto makes rugged ruts through fruit orchards.

Then in the Sierras, the *Vermont* twists and turns over mountains with steep, narrow roads. The car skids and slips on sandy, rocky ledges. Scary!

Next day, the long, dangerous journey of the Oregon desert begins. It's about three hundred miles of dry, parched land. Will they run out of water? Will they break down? Will they die in the desert?

The engine chokes, plugged with desert dust. Crocker tries to restart it. New batteries don't work.

From eight in the morning until four in the afternoon, they wait.
The sun blazes. They are hot and thirsty and tired and weak.

Wait! A man on horseback appears in the distance. Jackson fires his gun.

A cowboy gallops over and lassos the car. He pulls it to a small house.

Crocker works on the auto. The rancher offers his attic for the night.

What's that? On the side of the road?
A man with a bulldog!

The dog's name is Bud. The man
sells Bud to Jackson for fifteen
dollars. Jackson gets an unexpected
passenger and a good friend.

Bud rides in front and studies the road. Now the car isn't the only thing that's attracting attention. The goggles Bud wears to keep the dust and dirt out of his eyes even make a bulldog look cute.

That night all three sleep under the car. Bud snuggles up next to Jackson's sleeping bag for warmth.

Rain. Not just rain, but RAIN. The storm washes out the road.
The *Vermont* sinks into the mud.

They cut sagebrush and place it in front of the tires for traction.
Using a block and tackle, they haul the car out of the sticky,
oozing muck.

JUNE 21 ◦ TO ROCK SPRINGS, WYOMING

Jackson and Crocker are lost. The air is full of
mosquitoes. It's thirty-six hours since their last meal.
Hunger wears at them. Jackson looks at Bud. Crocker
looks at Bud. Bud licks them both.

Finally, a friendly sheepherder feeds them and shows them the railroad tracks. They follow the tracks toward Rock Springs.

The train brings a circus into Rock Springs. People think the *Vermont* is part of the show!

JUNE 23 • RAWLINS, WYOMING

A huge crowd greets them. Ladies ooh and ahh over Bud.

Children play fetch with him. They scratch his ears and his back. Bud stretches and croons and hams it up.

Men stroke their chins and say what a fine animal he is.

Bud agrees.

JULY 7 • TO NEBRASKA

Rain pelts Jackson, Crocker, and Bud.
Lightning flashes. Thunder roars.

Mud pulls the car in to the tops of the
wheels. The car is stuck eighteen times in
one day.

Dripping, bedraggled, and drenched.
Sopping, soggy, and soaked.

They detour north to find dry roads.

SMACK! Jackson rubs his head. **ZAp!** Something stings his face. **Ping! Ping!** What is hitting the car?

Crocker swats the air. It's raining. Not water—but flying grasshoppers! They lie so thick on the road that the tires can't tread. The *Vermont* stops. Insects pelt them like green hail.

People drive for miles to see the fantastic machine.

"Lordy, Harold, you ever see such a thing?"

"Hey, Ma, a devil wagon!"

People sit in trees for a good view.

A newspaper reports the *Vermont* whizzing through town non-stop at the breakneck speed of forty miles per hour. (That's no doubt an exaggeration, since a Winton's max was closer to thirty.)

JULY 17 © CHICAGO, ILLINOIS

Out of the small towns.
A big-time city!

Crowds gather around the *Vermont*, City officials shake the drivers' hands. Reporters clamor about. Cameras flash.

They spend the night in a real bed in a real hotel.

Zzzzz...

Next morning, about to leave . . .

Where's Bud?

People, people everywhere. But no Bud. They search over, under.

There! With the ladies in the fine hats! Bud, always the showoff, wandered where he'd get the most attention.

JULY 20 · CLEVELAND, OHIO

Winton Company, based in Cleveland, sees an opportunity for glory. It holds a banquet in Jackson's honor. Tables piled high with food stretch before the hungry and tired travelers. After the meager pickings on their journey, they've gone to feasting heaven.

A Winton boss says to his workers, "Boys, wash their car and make it look respectable!"

Jackson refuses, saying "I want mud from every state on this automobile."

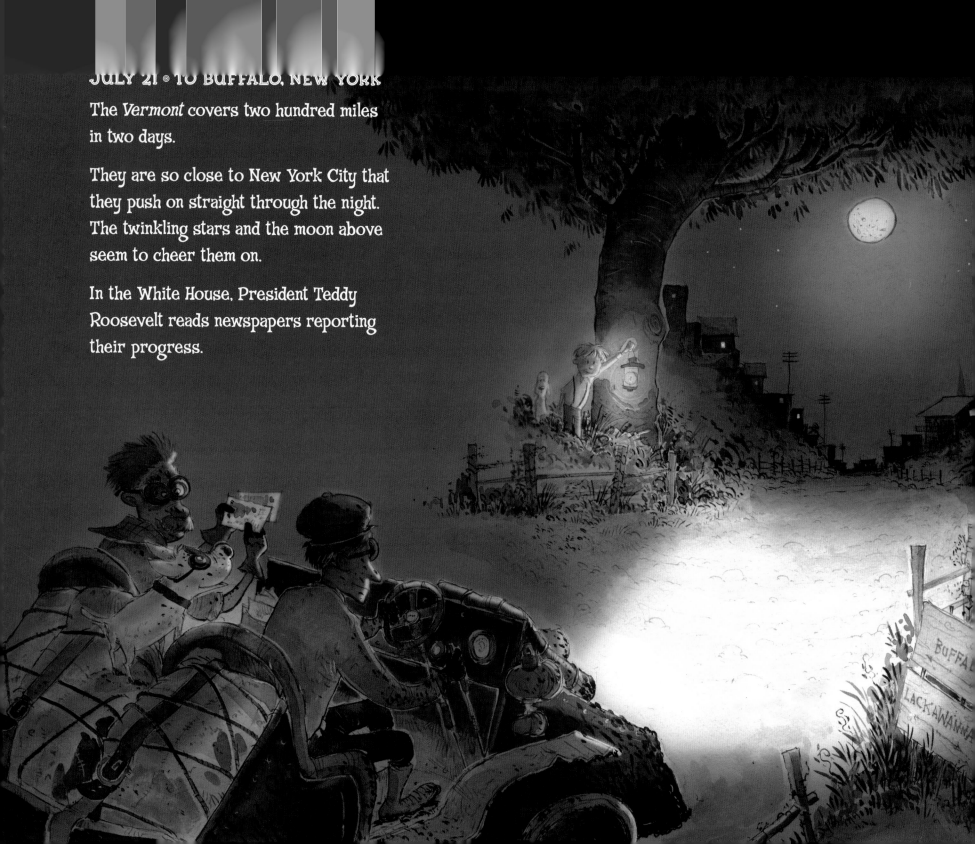

JULY 21 ○ TO BUFFALO, NEW YORK

The *Vermont* covers two hundred miles in two days.

They are so close to New York City that they push on straight through the night. The twinkling stars and the moon above seem to cheer them on.

In the White House, President Teddy Roosevelt reads newspapers reporting their progress.

A little before five o'clock in the morning, they make what will be their final tire repair by the lamplight's soft glow.

Jackson's wife, Bertha, arrives with friends and reporters. They hang a banner on the *Vermont*: "First Across the Continent—San Francisco to New York."

JULY 26 ◎ NEW YORK CITY

It's four thirty in the morning. Jackson, Crocker, and Bud drive the *Vermont* down Fifth Avenue.

The car is covered with mud. **Honk, Honk!**

Sixty-three days, twelve hours, and thirty minutes. About 5,600 miles of what passed for roads. About eight hundred gallons of gas. Eight thousand dollars of Jackson's own money.

All for a fifty-dollar bet that he never bothered to collect.

HONK

BEEP

HONK HONK

BEEP

AFTERWORD: THE STORY OF JACKSON AND BUD

The year 1903 was a big year for firsts in the United States. The Wright brothers invented the first flight-powered airplane, the first transatlantic cable was laid, the first wireless radio messages were sent to Europe—and Jackson, Crocker, and Bud completed the nation's first cross-country road trip.

Horatio Nelson Jackson was a doctor from Burlington, Vermont. He married Bertha Richardson Wells in 1899. Bertha was the daughter of one of the wealthiest businessmen in Vermont. At the time of the couple's 1903 visit to San Francisco, his wife had come into her inheritance, and

Bud guards the car as a crowd in Chicago takes a closer look.

Jackson had given up his medical practice, so he had the funds and the freedom to make this cross-country trip.

The 1903 Winton for which Jackson paid three thousand dollars already had 1,000 miles (1,609 km) on it. (In today's dollars, the car would cost seventy-three thousand dollars.) The Winton could attain a top speed of 30 miles (48 km) per hour.

Jackson hired Sewall J. Crocker as his mechanic and codriver. Crocker had been a professional bike racer in Tacoma, Washington, and was working in a San Francisco factory.

Optimistic Jackson, down-to-earth Crocker, and lovable Bud's exciting and humorous adventure lasted sixty-three days and took them over 5,600 miles (9,012 km) of roads, such as they were at the time. (There were only 150 miles (240 km) of paved roads in the entire United States! It would be another twenty years before a paved road, the Lincoln Highway, would connect San Francisco and

Jackson gives the *Vermont* a push in Wyoming.

Jackson drives with Crocker and Bud near the end of the trip.

New York.) There were no maps or road signs, and drivers often needed directions from locals to follow the roads. In the early 1900s, gas stations did not exist. Cars ran on fuel intended for stoves and farm machinery, which could be purchased at a general store.

Unbeknownst to Jackson and Crocker, on June 20, 1903, professional driver Tom Fetch and the *Automobile* magazine reporter Marius Krarup began a cross-country trip sponsored by the Packard Motor Car Company. On July 6 of the same year, Lester Whitman and Eugene Hammond, both well-qualified mechanics, joined what was becoming a cross-country contest, driving an Oldsmobile Runabout.

Which of the three automobiles won the unofficial race? In the end, the *Vermont* made it to New York City first in sixty-three days, twelve hours, and thirty minutes, making their journey the nation's first successful cross-country road trip. But Fetch and Krarup completed their trip in a day and a half less. Whitman and Hammond were out of the running in both categories, being the last to arrive and logging a total time of seventy-two days, twenty-one hours and thirty minutes.

At the advanced age of forty-five, Jackson insisted upon enlisting in World War I (1914–1918) as a battlefield surgeon. Badly wounded at the Battle of Argonne in France, he returned to Vermont as a hero, having received the United States' Distinguished Service Cross and France's Croix de Guerre medal.

Sewall Crocker used his temporary fame to look for sponsorship for an auto tour. He eventually made a tour of Europe. Suffering from a nervous condition and general ill health, he died in his hometown of Tacoma, Washington, at the age of thirty-two.

Bud joined the Jacksons and their two daughters for a long and happy life as their family dog.

In 1944 Jackson donated the *Vermont*, his scrapbook, and Bud's goggles to the Smithsonian Institution in Washington, D.C., where they are still on display. Horatio Nelson Jackson died in 1955 at the age of eighty-two.

Bud poses in his goggles.

BIBLIOGRAPHY

Duncan, Dayton. *Horatio's Drive, America's First Road Trip.* Directed by Ken Burns. American Lives II Film Project. First broadcast on PBS, October 2003.

Duncan, Dayton, and Ken Burns. *Horatio's Drive: America's First Road Trip.* New York: Alfred A. Knopf, 2003.

Hill, Ralph Nading. *The Mad Doctor's Drive: Being an Account of the 1st Auto Trip across the U.S.A., San Francisco to New York, 1903; or, Sixty-Three Days on a Winton Motor Carriage.* Brattleboro, VT: Stephen Greene Press, 1964.

McConnell, Curt. *Coast to Coast by Automobile: The Pioneering Trips, 1899–1908.* Stanford, CA: Stanford University Press, 2000.

FURTHER READING

Bendick, Jeanne. *Eureka! It's an Automobile!* Minneapolis: Millbrook Press, 1992.

Blumberg, Rhoda. *The Incredible Journey of Lewis and Clark.* New York: Lothrop, Lee & Shepherd, 1987.

Brooke, Lindsay. *Ford Model T: The Car That Put the World on Wheels.* Saint Paul: Motorbooks, 2008.

Callan, Jim. *America in the 1900s and 1910s.* New York: Facts on File, 2006.

Conley, Robyn. *The Automobile.* Danbury, CT: Franklin Watts, 2005.

Cunningham, Kevin. *The History of the Automobile.* Chanhassen, MN: Child's World, 2005.

Dooling, Michael. *The Great Horse-less Carriage Race.* New York: Holiday House, 2002.

Sharman, Margaret. *The 1900s: The First Decade.* Austin, TX: Raintree Steck-Vaughn, 1994.

Time-Life Books. *Dawn of the Century 1900–1910.* Alexandria, VA: Time-Life Books, 1998.

WEBSITES

PBS
http://www.pbs.org/horatio/index.html
A retelling of Horatio's story based on the PBS film *Horatio's Drive*. The site includes a map of the trip, information about the Winton, resources for educators, and an automobile chronology.

San Francisco Chronicle
http://www.sfgate.com/cgi-bin/article.cgi?f=/c/a/2003/06/16/MN281103.DTL
An article about a June 2003 re-creation of Jackson's trip.

Smithsonian Institution America on the Move
http://americanhistory.si.edu/onthemove/exhibition/
Explore #1, Transportation in America, for information on what driving was like before Jackson's trip; #5, People on the Move tells more about Jackson's life before and after his journey; and #7, Crossing the Country, offers some details about the Winton as well as the trip. And there's a good picture of Bud's goggles.

University of Texas State Maps
http://www.lib.utexas.edu/maps/map_sites/states_sites.html
Find links to maps of U.S. states and territories.

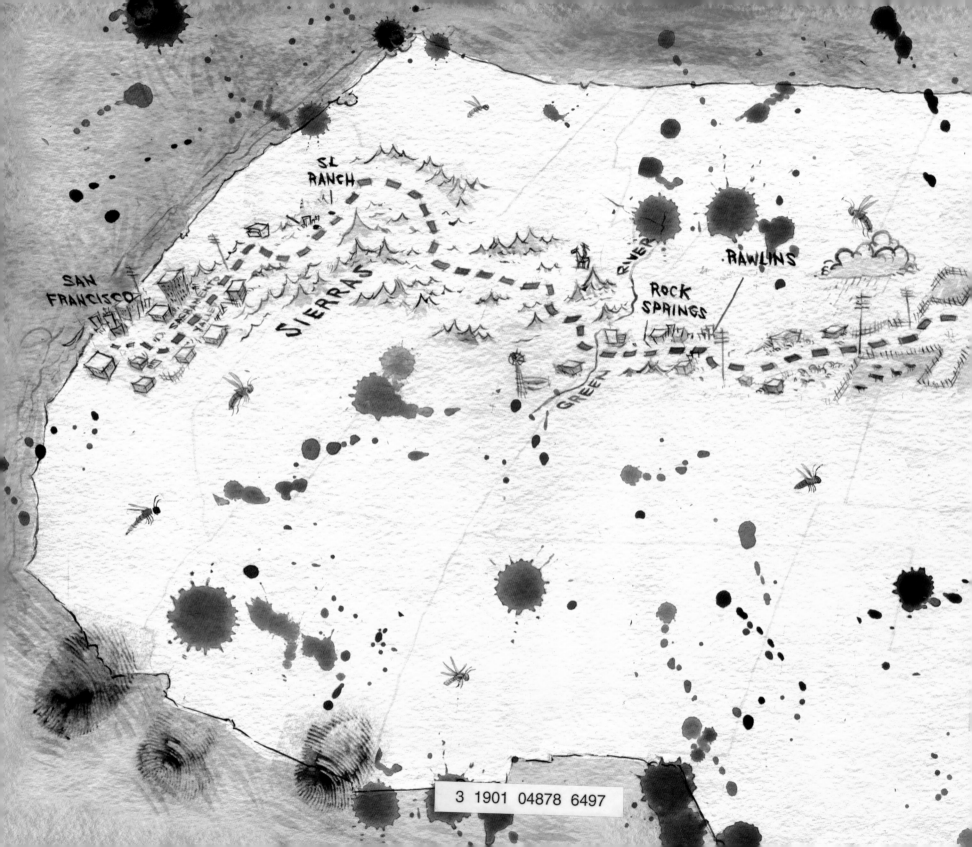

SAN FRANCISCO

SL RANCH

SIERRAS

SACRAMENTO VALLEY

ROCK SPRINGS

GREEN RIVER

RAWLINS